To D[...]

Happy [...] y-
Maybe there will be
some thoughts in here
that will help you
with the perplexing
job of being a Mother.
I love you —
Mother

God
can handle it
. . . Day by Day

Dr. S. M. Henriques

BRIGHTON BOOKS
Nashville, TN 37205
1--800-256-8584

ISBN 1-887655-94-8

The quoted ideas expressed in this book (but not Scripture verses) are not, in all cases, exact quotations, as some have been edited for clarity and brevity. In all cases, the author has attempted to maintain the speaker's original intent. In some cases, quoted material for this book was obtained from secondary sources, primarily print media. While every effort was made to ensure the accuracy of these sources, the accuracy cannot be guaranteed. For additions, deletions, corrections or clarifications in future editions of this text, please write BRIGHTON BOOKS.

Printed in the United States of America.

Layout by Swan Lake Communications, Jackson, Mississippi
Cover Design by Criswell Freeman

For the loving church family of
Bethlehem Baptist Church,
Benton, Mississippi,
and
my wonderful friends at
Baptist Book Store
(Lifeway Christian Resources),
Jackson, Mississippi:

God brought us together
at just the right time!

I thank my God every
time I remember you.
Philippians 1:3

There is no impossible situation that God cannot handle. He won't necessarily handle it your way, but He'll handle it.

Charles R. Swindoll

You have not measured
your fingers with God's,
therefore you cannot
know what is in store.

Lithuanian proverb

Introduction

Okay, admit it: Life is not exactly what you had in mind. It hasn't played out according to the script, has it? Well, not *our* script, anyway.

The truth is, we don't always know what we need anyway. Life sometimes is too confusing, too busy, too loud, too — real. When we try to take matters into our own hands, we soon discover that we can't handle it.

But *God* can handle it! He wrote the script, and He is quite capable of handling anything that comes, every day that comes.

Arriving at the place where we can honestly believe that God can handle whatever comes requires that we pull a few things into perspective. Seeing things the way God sees them makes a big difference in our approach to life — even if it doesn't turn out the way we thought it would.

Then, with a new focus, we make fresh discoveries about God, ourselves, and the world He made. Whatever we face, God can handle it.

Ah, Sovereign Lord . . .
nothing is too hard for you.
Jeremiah 32:17

No created being can ever know
how much and how sweetly
and tenderly God loves him.

Julian of Norwich

We are not what He wants us to be,
but we are not unwanted.

David Roper

Our only warrant for believing that
God cares is that He has communicated
this fact to us. It is the key fact
about Himself which He has chosen
to reveal to us, and it is the most
comforting fact imaginable.

Louis Cassels

*How great is the love the Father
has lavished on us, that we
should be called children of God!*
1 John 3:1

He *Said* He Loves Us!

Mary Shawnhan-Knight wrote in *Christian Herald* magazine several years ago of the antics of her children one night at bedtime. She was not amused by their tactics to keep from going to sleep. As a result, the oldest daughter became upset and began crying.

The mother went back into the room and asked, "Karen, what is the matter?" The little girl sobbed, "Do you still love me?"

Her mom replied, "Of course I still love you, but I do get cross when you don't do what I ask you to do." She closed the door, but the crying continued.

Mrs. Knight was just about to go back into the bedroom, when the younger child, only four years old at the time, said, "Be quiet, Karen. She *said* she loves us, didn't she?"

We may feel sometimes as if God doesn't love us. But instead of whimpering in the dark, we can remind ourselves that God really does love us.

After all, He *said* He did!

It is in the deepest darkness of the starless midnight that men learn how to hold on to the hidden Hand most tightly and how that Hand holds them; that He sees where we do not, and knows the way He takes; and though the way be to us a roundabout way, it is the right way.

A. T. Pierson

Blessed is the man who perseveres under trial.
James 1:12

Swimming in the Dark

In May 1997, Susan Maroney became the first woman to swim the 118 miles from Cuba to Florida. In her third attempt, the 22-year-Australian swam for 24½ hours in shark-infested waters, surrounded by a 28-by-8-foot shark-proof cage. The cage was itself attached to an escort boat moving alongside her.

When Maroney reached Fort Zachary State Park in the Florida Keys, she was badly sunburned, dehydrated and covered with welts from jellyfish stings.

At one time, she had hallucinations, in which she thought she saw monkeys hanging on the cage.

She stated afterwards, "So many times you think, 'I just don't want to keep going.' " She was encouraged by her mother and brother, who motivated her from the escort boat during the night.

Swimming in the night, by the way, was what Maroney described as "the hardest part."

Have you ever felt as if you were swimming in the dark? Perhaps, growing weary, you've felt like giving up. Here are a few things we can learn from Susan Maroney's experience:

(1) Work hard to accomplish your dreams.

(2) Surround yourself with people who believe in you and will stay with you, even during the "dark" times.

(3) Keep your goal in sight, even if you imagine things that aren't there.

Above everything else, *keep swimming!*

I've never met anyone who became instantly mature. It's a painstaking process that God takes us through, and it includes such things as waiting, failing, losing, and being misunderstood — each calling for extra doses of perseverance.

Charles R. Swindoll

The silent power of perseverance grows irresistibly greater with time.

Goethe

Those who turn back know only the ordeal, but they who persevere remember the adventure.

Milo L. Arnold

Bear in mind, if you are going to amount to anything, that your success does not depend upon the brilliancy and the impetuousity with which you take hold, but upon the bull-doggedness with which you hang on after you have taken hold.

A. B. Meldrum

Fall seven times, stand up eight.

Japanese proverb

Let us not become weary in doing good, for at the proper time we will reap a harvest if we do not give up.
Galatians 6:9

On days when life is difficult and I feel
overwhelmed, as I do fairly often, it
helps to remember in my prayers that
all God requires of me is to trust Him
and be His friend. I find I can do that.

Bruce Larson

God is too kind to do anything cruel . . .
too wise to make a mistake . . .
too deep to explain Himself.

Charles Swindoll

There is no greater joy than the peace
and assurance of knowing that,
whatever the future may hold, you are
secure in the loving arms of the Savior.

Billy Graham

*But you are to hold fast to the Lord your
God, as you have until now.*
Joshua 23:8

Turning the Light On

Imagine walking through a dark room, and sharply bumping your legs on the furniture. In a situation like that, the furniture is nothing more than an obstacle which must be avoided.

Once you switch on a light, everything is different. The sharp corner which gouged out your shin is actually a beautiful table, its oak grain richly polished and the top ready for service. That obstacle which almost tripped you is a comfortable wingback chair, in just the right position for quiet moments of reading or prayer.

Much of life is like that. When we are in the darkness of discouragement, we don't see the things that might trip or bruise. When we are hurting, we don't understand that the thing that caused the pain may have a much greater purpose than we have experienced.

It takes the illumination that faith brings to reveal the true purpose our Father has. In your life — are those *really* obstacles, or would the light of God show them to be something else?

The light shines in the darkness . . . .
John 1:5

Sometimes God sends the brilliant
light of a rainbow to remind us of His
presence, lest we forget in our personal
darkness His great and gracious
promises to never leave us alone.

Verdell Davis

Have you ever taken your fears to God,
got the horizons of Eternity about them,
and looked at them in the light
of His love and grace?

Robert J. McCracken

Thank the Lord, it is His love that
arranges our tomorrows — and we may
be certain that whatever tomorrow
brings, His love sent it our way.

Charles Swindoll

The Lord is with me, I will not be afraid.
Psalm 118:6

It's Me and I'm Scared

A little boy had a part in the school Christmas play. He had one small line, which he and his dad had rehearsed numerous times. He had it down perfectly.

But when the time arrived to make his entrance on the stage, the little fellow suddenly became very afraid. He was supposed to say, "It is I; be not afraid."

Instead, it came out as "It's me, and I'm scared."

We know how he felt, don't we? Maybe it wasn't because we've been in a play when we forgot our lines. But each of us have been there where we knew all the right answers and were afraid anyway.

Charlie Brown once said in a *Peanuts* comic strip, "I have a new philosophy: I'm only going to dread one day at a time."

We could try that. A better way: hear God say, "It's Me, and I'm God. Trust Me."

When I am afraid, I will trust in you.
Psalm 56:3

Have courage for the sorrows of life and
patience for the small ones; and when
you have laboriously accomplished
your daily task, go to sleep in peace.
God is awake.

Victor Hugo

Find a purpose in life so big
it will challenge every capacity
to be at your best.

David O. McKay

Leave the broken, irreversible past
in God's hands, and step out into
the invincible future with Him.

Oswald Chambers

Increase our faith.
Luke 17:5

What Shape Is Your Pumpkin?

A farmer once went to the county fair with a pumpkin that was the exact shape and size of a two-gallon jug. It was so unusual that his pumpkin won the blue ribbon.

When asked how he got a pumpkin to grow like that, the farmer replied, "It was easy. As soon as it started to grow, I stuck it inside a two-gallon jug."

If your faith was a thing you could hold in your hand, and you had put it into a container when it was still very, very small, what would it look like now? What shape would it have taken by now?

Is it the shape of an aspirin bottle? A fifty-gallon drum? As you've seen challenges to your faith, you were able to believe in the promises of God — at least to a point. Then came the day when you were challenged beyond the capacity even of the fifty-gallon drum. Your faith had gone as it could.

Here's a better comparison: your faith may be the exact shape and size of an egg. And when that faith began to develop and expand, you soon found that eggshell too confining. You stretched and opened yourself to the bright and glorious promises of God. As you grew, you discovered that shell was too fragile to hold your faith inside. The eggshell cracked open, and your faith continues to grow, without being restrained by any container.

We must go beyond positive thinking and self-reinforcement. Is your faith confined to imaginary containers, or is it free to roam and explore the tremendous will and blessings of God?

Christ wants not nibblers of the possible, but grabbers of the impossible.

C. T. Studd

We have a God who
delights in impossibilities.

Andrew Murray

Either He is in charge, or He is not.

Elisabeth Elliot

Beware of cut-and-dried theologies that
reduce the ways of God to a manageable
formula that keeps life safe. God often
does the unexplainable just to keep us
on our toes — and also on our knees.

Warren Wiersbe

*Trust in the Lord forever, for the Lord, the
Lord, is the Rock eternal.*
Isaiah 26:4

You can come out of
the furnace of trouble
two ways: if you let
it consume you,
you come out a cinder;
but there is a kind of
metal which refuses
to be consumed,
and comes out a star.

Jean Church

*But he knows the way that I take; when he
has tested me, I will come forth as gold.*
Job 23:10

A Boiled Egg or a Potato

Sorrow can either make us bitter and hard, or it can make us softer and more sympathetic. Billie Wilcox wrote in *Guideposts* several years ago of the time she and her husband Frank were living in Pakistan. Their six-month-old baby died while they were there, and an old Punjabi came to comfort them.

He told them, "A tragedy like this is similar to being plunged into boiling water. If you are an egg, your affliction will make you hard-boiled and unresponsive. If you are a potato, you will emerge soft and pliable, resilient and adaptable."

Mrs. Wilcox wrote in response, "It may sound funny to God, but there have been many times when I have prayed, 'O Lord, let me be a potato.' "

It doesn't sound funny at all! Deep inside, we know that our reaction to difficulty can sometimes make all the difference. Will we come out of it hard and bitter, or soft and sensitive to the Spirit of God?

I have tested you in the furnace of affliction.
Psalm 56:3

God never wastes a "wait."
Jan Carlberg

Not so in haste, my heart;
Have faith in God, and wait;
Although He linger long,
He never comes too late.
Unknown

Waiting seems to be a kind of acted-out
prayer that is required more often
and honored more often than I could
understand until I saw what remarkable
faith-muscles this act develops.
Catherine Marshall

Blessed are all who wait for him.
Isaiah 30:18b

The Waiting Time

Louis XIV, king of France, ordered a coach brought to the front door of his residence one day. When the coach pulled up in the nick of time, the king is reported to have said, "I almost had to wait."

Sometimes we think waiting would be the worst possible thing. The waiting time can be agony.

When we are anxious for God to act, it may seem that everything has come to a complete standstill. We wonder why God doesn't move faster. Why doesn't God *do* something — *now?*

Waiting has never been easy. Perhaps that's why the Scriptures encourage us to "wait upon the Lord" as much as they do. During a particularly trying time in his life, the psalmist wrote, "Be still before the Lord and wait patiently for him. . . ." (Psalm 37:7).

While you think God is wasting time, it may very well be that the waiting is the thing He has for you. There may be a very important lesson to learn in the waiting time.

So, what are *you* waiting for?

God gives every bird its food, but He
does not throw it into the nest.
Josiah Gilbert Holland

Lift up your eyes. Your heavenly Father
waits to bless you—in inconceivable
ways to make your life what you
never dreamed it could be.
Anne Ortlund

Joy is like a well containing sweet water.
It is not enough to know the water is
there or even to drill the well. If the
well is to be useful, the water must be
brought to the surface. Those who know
Christ have found the source of joy.
Ron Hembree

*Many are the plans in a man's heart, but it
is the Lord's purpose that prevails.*
Proverbs 19:21

The Pump-Priming Principle

When I was a small boy, our family often would drive out into the country where my father's family owned a farm. I was fascinated by the old farm house. Dad had worked hard to modernize that house, including adding the convenience of indoor plumbing.

For years, the house was supplied by an old, hand-operated pump by the back porch. To this day, I remember the groans which filled the air whenever the handle was worked up and down.

Dad showed me how to "prime" the pump by first pouring a little water in the top, so it would pull the water up from the well far below.

The "Pump-Priming Principle" says that ordinarily, great things do not just happen to us. We must be prepared — primed — before we can be receptive to the things God wants to do in our lives.

Occasionally, the "priming" even includes things that we would not have chosen for ourselves. But that's the only way the cool water of our souls can rise to the top.

God may be priming your life right now for something wonderful He's about to do for you!

God's silence is in no way indicative of His activity or involvement in our lives. He may be silent but He is not still.

Charles Stanley

Wait for God, even if the night seems dark. He will give you everything you need when you need it.

Peter Wallace

God never hurries. There are no deadlines against which He must work. To know this is to quiet our spirits and relax our nerves.

A. W. Tozer

I wait for the Lord, my soul waits, and in his word I put my hope.
Psalm 130:5

Hurry Up, God!

Phillips Brooks was known throughout the English-speaking world in the 19th century as "a prince of preachers." We know him as the man who wrote the familiar Christmas carol, *O Little Town of Bethlehem.*

One day Brooks was pacing the floor like a caged lion. One of his friends asked him, "What is the trouble?"

"The trouble," replied Brooks, "is that I'm in a hurry, but God isn't."

Oswald Chambers gave us this word of encouragement:

"Watch God's way in your life, and you will find He is developing you as He does the trees and flowers, a deep silent working of the God of Creation."

Stop pacing. He is working, and He knows what He is doing.

God is never in a hurry.

Henri Nouwen

There are things to be seen and learned in apparent wastelands which cannot be seen and learned in places of comfort, convenience and company. God intends to keep us in a place where there is nothing else we can count on.

Elisabeth Elliot

We trust in the living God.
1 Timothy 4:10 (KJV)

We Need Nothing Else

Sir Christopher Wren was commissioned to design the great Corn Market in Windsor, England. His first design was rejected because it showed no pillars holding up the roof. He explained the pillars would not be needed, but the city fathers couldn't conceive of such a thing. They insisted that pillars should be added to the design.

Some time after the building was constructed, it was discovered that Sir Wren had won his argument after all. He had made each of the pillars one-half inch shorter than the roof. There they stand, but they serve no purpose, and the roof has never sagged.

We are the same way. If we live in Christ, we don't need the many things we use as pillars to support our lives. Our support is dependent on the basic structure and nature of our relationship with Christ. Paul wrote in 2 Corinthians 3:5, ". . . our sufficiency is of God" (KJV).

C. S. Lewis wrote, "He who has God and many other things, has no more than he who has God alone."

What do you need?

Sometimes our light goes out but is blown into flame by another human being. Each of us owes deepest thanks to those who have rekindled this light.

Albert Schweitzer

Be still, and in the quiet moments, listen to the voice of your heavenly Father. His words can renew your spirit. No one knows you and your needs like He does.

Janet L. Weaver

To cultivate serenity, it is imperative that we guard the discipline of solitude.

Charles Swindoll

You, O Lord, keep my lamp burning.
Psalm 18:28

Keeping Your Torch Lit

Officials reported that as the date for the 1998 Winter Olympics drew nearer, those running with the Olympic Torch were having trouble keeping the fire burning. It was a troublesome problem from the beginning.

So they came out with a new torch, redesigned to better protect the flame from the wind. But as the torch *came* out, the flame *went* out.

Ever felt that way? Certainly there are periods when it becomes increasingly difficult to keep the fires of faithfulness and diligence burning brightly. We go about our duties, perhaps without even realizing that our torches have gone out.

When this happens, we need to follow the example of those running with the Olympic Torch: stop long enough to relight.

It may require something as simple as a day off, a good night's rest, a refocusing of priorities, time alone with God — or maybe something more involved.

Think: What might be necessary to start the fires burning brightly again in your heart?

The God of Israel, the Savior, is sometimes a God that hides Himself but never a God that is absent; sometimes in the dark, but never at a distance.

Matthew Henry

My Presence will go with you,
and I will give you rest.
Exodus 33:14

That Sure Helps!

It was "Ask the Pastor" Day in Sunday School, and the pastor stopped by the first grade department. There were a lot of questions, some of them thoughtful, some of them silly.

Just what you might expect from the typical group of first graders.

Then one bright fellow asked, "Did Jesus ever have to go to school?" The pastor replied, "Certainly. He grew up just like any other boy and had the same problems you have."

The little boy sighed. "Boy! That sure helps!"

Doesn't it? To know that He has experienced what we have, that He has walked through some dark valleys Himself, that He has been misunderstood, hated, used and even killed — helps us in what we face from day to day.

With God, go over the sea —
Without Him, not
over the threshold.

Russian proverb

We are lifted above our circumstances
when we look into the face of Jesus
Gigi Graham Tchividjian

You have never tested God's
resources until you have
attempted the impossible.
Unknown

Dear Lord,
never let me be afraid
to pray for the impossible.
Dorothy Shellenberger

*Trust in the Lord with all your heart, and
lean not on your own understanding.*
Proverbs 3:5

Impala Christians

The impala is a member of the antelope family and roams freely in Africa. It is a magnificent creature. It can jump to a height of over ten feet, and cover thirty feet in one horizontal jump. In spite of its remarkable ability to jump, the African impala can be kept in an enclosure in any zoo with a three-foot wall.

The reason is simple: they won't jump if they cannot see where their feet will land.

Sometimes we don't obey Christ because we can't, with all our reason, knowledge and experience, figure out where our feet will land. Instead, we stay cooped up in tiny cages of our own making, cages that in actuality should be no challenge at all.

We are unwilling to jump, but God says, *"You may not be able to see over the three-foot wall, but I can! Jump!"*

He tells us over and over again in His Word that He is a God who can be trusted. In fact, that is what the Bible is about! We can trust Him to provide a way through the confusion of our lives and the muck of our sin.

Jump! Jump into His arms. He'll catch you.

Be absolutely certain
that our Lord loves you,
devotedly and individually,
loves you just as you are. . . .
Accustom yourself to the
wonderful thought that God
loves you with a tenderness,
a generosity, and an
intimacy that surpasses
all your dreams.

Abbe Henri de Tourville

Search me, O God, and know my heart;
test me and know my anxious thoughts.
Psalm 139:23

The Crack in the Line

As we prepared for a family gathering around the Fourth of July one year, I rolled the gas grill over to begin cooking. But I discovered that the tank was empty. That seemed strange, since I didn't think we had used that much. My first thought was that there was a leak somewhere.

We had an extra tank, so I pulled it over and connected it to the grill. When all the connections were tight, I turned the valve on the top of the grill. I heard a sound which revealed where the problem was: the brass connection which held the hose from the tank into the bottom of the grill had a hairline crack in it. It was there all along, but I could not find it until the pressurized gas flowed through it.

With great love and care, our wise Heavenly Father knows exactly what we need to go through in order to show us where the "cracks" are.

But not just so we can know where they are. He does it so we can do something about them.

Now you're cookin'.

When things happen which dismay we ought to look to God for His meaning, remembering that He is not taken by surprise nor can His purposes be thwarted in the end.

Elisabeth Elliot

Sometimes when you take another look, you will find something to be grateful for that you might otherwise have overlooked.

Timothy Miller

The discovery of God lies in the daily and the ordinary, not in the spectacular and the heroic. If we cannot find God in the routines of home and shop, then we will not find Him at all.

Richard J. Foster

. . . the Lord your God will be with you wherever you go.
Joshua 1:9b

John Henry

Once upon a time, a man owned a race horse. He didn't see much potential in that animal as a money-maker, so he sold him for $1,000. The new owner sold him for $2,000.

The third owner did even better, selling the horse for $10,000. The fourth owner soon took advantage of an opportunity to trade the horse for two quality horses. The fifth owner decided there wasn't enough potential to bother.

Finally, someone took a risk, buying the horse that nobody wanted — for $25,000.

The horse was known as John Henry, and he became the leading money-maker in 1981. When he was eventually retired from racing, he had been credited with earning more than six million dollars during his career.

Six men had owned a winning race horse and didn't realize what they had.

Do you know what you have? As followers of Christ, we have so many more resources than we realize.

Let us determine that, regardless of what life brings, we will do our best to discover the glorious treasures Christ offers us for living.

Keep on going and chances
are you will stumble on
something, perhaps when you
are least expecting it.
I have never heard of anyone
stumbling on something
sitting down.

Charles F. Kettering

The blessing of the Lord brings wealth,
and he adds no trouble to it.
Proverbs 10:22

Worthless Black Sand

Leadville, California, was a small, quiet town until thousands of men swarmed in with their panning tins, looking for their fortunes in the gold rush in the 1860s. Almost overnight the little village became a boom town, bustling with life and excitement. But just sixteen years later, abandoned cabins and sluice boxes were all that was left.

Veteran prospectors had come to Leadville in great numbers, but soon left discouraged. There was a little gold in the nearby gulch, for sure. But the abundant black sand gummed up the riffles in the sluice boxes. Holes dug for panning gold would fill in with the sand. That black sand stained everything it touched. The prospectors cursed the sand and moved on.

Two men, William Stevens and Alvinus Wood, were convinced that gold was still there near Leadville. They began buying up old abandoned claims. They quickly found a little gold, so their expectations heightened. But soon they, too, began to have problems with the black sand. It looked as though Stevens and Wood would have to abandon their dreams.

One day Stevens decided to send a sample of the black sand back East for analysis. When the report came back, the men were surprised to learn that the seemingly worthless black sand was actually lead carbonate — loaded with silver! The two opened the Rock Mine, the first producing silver mine in the entire district. In a few short years they were fabulously rich.

That black sand, which prospectors had cursed as being the only insurmountable obstacle in their search for riches, contained materials that would have made them luxuriantly wealthy. They were looking for flecks of gold, without realizing that what they had was worth far more. They didn't know what they had.

Do you realize what you have? Do you realize that the awesome, majestic, sweet presence of Christ in our lives opens up other resources to us we could not have otherwise? Sometimes in our haste to find easy answers for our problems, we are guilty of looking for tiny flecks of gold compared to what God wants to give us.

Isn't it time we stopped looking for simple solutions when God longs to give us far more?

The Sovereign Lord is my strength;
he makes my feet like the feet of a deer.
Habakkuk 3:19a

God is thinking about you personally,
and is planning for you in ways that
you could never understand,
let alone imagine.
Let Him have His way.

Warren Wiersbe

Seize today. Live for today.
Wring it dry of every opportunity.

John Haggai

Do not follow where the path may lead.
Follow God, instead, to where there is
no path and leave a trail.

Unknown

*Have faith in the Lord your God
and you will be upheld.*
2 Chronicles 20:20

The shepherd isn't always out in front, leading his sheep. In the lengthening twilight, when the sheep must pass through the darkest shadows in the deepest wadis the shepherd drops back and walks with them.

Ray Vander Laan

From my earliest days I have treasured His unforsaking presence. It conquers the storms of my life.

Calvin Miller

We can go through all the activities of our days in joyful awareness of God's presence with whispered prayers of praise and adoration flowing continuously from our hearts.

Richard J. Foster

. . . they will call him "Immanuel" — which means "God with us."
Matthew 1:23

Jesus' *Other* Name

Do you recognize the names of Nathan Birnbaum, Francis Octavia Smith or Archibald Leach? No?

Those are the birth names of George Burns, Dale Evans and Cary Grant. They each changed their names at some point in their lives for one reason or another.

Other examples are Gerald Ford (Leslie Lynch King, Jr.), John Denver (Henry John Deutschendorf, Jr.), and John Wayne (Marion Michael Morrison).

Jesus Christ had another name, too. But it wasn't one given to Him because the name "Jesus" was unsatisfactory. It was given to Him because of the added significance it would carry.

That other Name was "Immanuel," which is Hebrew for "God with us."

Think of that! We have the wonderful assurance that God is with us through His Son Jesus Christ. He is with us in trouble, loneliness, bereavement — and a host of other situations in which we may find ourselves.

Most new discoveries are suddenly-seen
things that were always there.

Susanne K. Langer

The simplest and commonest
truth seems new and wonderful
when we experience it for the
first time in our own lives.

Marie von Ebner-Eschenbach

Miracles are nothing other than
God's advancing truth seen
with surprised eyes.

Gerald G. May

*When they saw the star,
they were overjoyed.*
Matthew 2:10

Holy Ground Moments

The wonder of that night never lost its brilliance for them. For years after they first heard the angels announce the birth of Jesus, the shepherds probably told and retold the story.

They may have said something like, "It was a night just like this one, when we were watching over the flocks during the night. We were standing right about where you are right now, when suddenly we were bathed and surrounded by an overwhelming Light, the glory of which we had never seen before."

They would go on to describe as best they could the appearance of the first angel, and the impact of his words on them. They would tell of their hurried trip to Bethlehem, and of their discovery of the baby in the manger, just as the angel had said.

The commonplace was glorified in the sense that God was present in the midst of their routine as never before. It was "holy ground."

These types of experiences are not limited to those times when the Bible is open on our laps. They do not come only when we are praying alone in the woods, while watching a beautiful sunrise, or only in the church building on Sunday.

In fact, if our relationships with Christ are real at all, holy ground moments will happen even in the routine of our lives. When we have just one of these holy ground moments with God, the rest of life takes on a sparkling freshness.

It is the sparkling presence of God that sparkles and glimmers and dances through our lives.

The shepherds went back to the routine of tending their sheep. Yet they never got over it. May we each have such an experience with God — a "holy ground moment" — that we never get over it.

Give me, O God, this day a strong and vivid sense that Thou art by my side.

John Baillie

. . . all who heard it were amazed at what the shepherds said to them.
Luke 2:18

The world will never starve for wonders
but only for the lack of wonder.
G. K. Chesterton

Miracles and wonders are the
ordinary stuff of God's day.
Jan Carlberg

There is a great deal more to be gotten
out of things than is generally gotten out
of them, whether the thing be a chapter
of the Bible or a yellow turnip.
George MacDonald

But Mary treasured up all these things and
pondered them in her heart.
Luke 2:19

Look for the light of God that is hitting your life, and you will find sparkles you didn't know were there.

Barbara Johnson

You are resplendent with light . . . .
Psalm 76:4a

The Sparkling Presence of God

We live on a small lake. It's not a paradise, but there are many times God has used the sights, sounds and smells of our lake to calm my spirit and remind me of His presence.

In the winter months, in the early afternoon, the sun is at just the right position and angle to create some eye-catching special effects. The sunlight bouncing off the water makes the lake come alive, as the water sparkles and dances. The entire lake looks as though it were covered with diamonds!

Along that same line, Leslie Williams, in her book *Night Wrestling*, wrote: "If we train ourselves, we can sense God's presence in every object or person we encounter during even a humdrum day; and recognizing the sparkle in the bubble is itself a way to worship the God who created bubbles and added sparkles for the fun of it."

If we are careful to watch for them, we will see the sparkles that God puts in front of us every day, every moment.

Aren't they beautiful?

What can be more foolish than to
think that all this rare fabric of heaven
and earth could come by chance,
when all the skill of science is not
able to make an oyster.

Jeremy Taylor

Look at the stars. The most universally
awesome experience that mankind
knows is to stand alone on a clear night
and look at the stars. It was God
who first set the stars in space;
He is their Maker and Master —
they are all in His hands and
subject to His will.
Such are His power and His majesty.

J. I. Packer

The heavens praise your wonders, O Lord.
Psalm 89:5

Keeping It In Focus

Charles Haddon Spurgeon wrote many years ago:

"There is no place where God is not. God is there in a thousand wonders, upholding rocky barriers, filling the buttercups with their perfume and refreshing the lonely pines with the breath of his mouth. Descend . . . into the lowest depths of the ocean, where undisturbed water sleeps, and the very sand is motionless in unbroken quiet, but the glory of the Lord is there, revealing its excellence in the silent palace of the sea. Borrow the wings of the morning and fly to the uttermost parts of the sea, but God is there."

His beauty is stamped in all of creation:
The glory of God can be seen
from the smallest raindrop
to the mighty flash of lightning;
from the tiny rosebud
to the huge magnolia blossom;
from the rich, fertile soil of the Mississippi
Delta to the arid, dusty land of the desert.
We can see His stamp of glory in all the world,
from the music of a sparkling brook
to the majestic tumbling waterfall;

from the gnarled, gentle hands of
a loving grandfather
to the birth-fresh fragility
of a baby's fingernail;
from the silence of the stars
to the peal of thunder;
from the mirror-like smoothness
of a placid lake
to the wind-driven thunderous waves
smashing on the shore.

In the fresh greenery of the spring; in the dazzling color of autumn; in the joy of discovery on a baby's face; and in the fulfillment and meaning of the New Birth, we can see the glory of God.

When we focus on the glorious things He has done, everything suddenly drops into focus. When we meditate on the aroma of the earth in the spring, and how different it is then than in the fall; when we consider the mystery and attraction of human love, and how it mirrors the eternal love of our Heavenly Father; when we contemplate the intricacies of the human body — those are the times we realize that God is much, much bigger than the things which cause us so much grief in the first place.

You can revive your sense
of wonder by merely
saying to yourself:
Suppose this were the only
time. Suppose this sunset, this
moonrise, this symphony,
this buttered toast, this
sleeping child, this flag
against the sky . . .
suppose you would never
experience these things again!
Arthur Gordon

*I will meditate on all your works and
consider all your mighty deeds.*
Psalm 77:12

Get the right perspective.
When Goliath came against the
Israelites, the soldiers all thought,
"He's so big we can never kill him."
David looked at the same giant and
thought, "He's so big I can't miss."
Russ Johnston

One of God's most majestic creatures
challenges us to look at our difficulties
from a broader perspective—
the soaring eagle never worries
how he will cross a raging river.
Roy Lessin

One must wait until the evening to see
how splendid the day has been.
Sophocles

*Cast your cares on the Lord
and he will sustain you.*
Psalm 55:22

When It Gets Dark Enough

Three men were visiting the Grand Canyon for the first time. One of them was an artist, another a pastor, and the third was a cowboy. As they stood on the edge of the Canyon, each one responded differently.

The artist exclaimed, "What a beautiful scene to paint!" The minister said, "What a wonderful example of the handiwork of God!"

The cowboy mused, "What a terrible place to lose a cow!"

A little boy ran into the house and begged his dad to come see a strange dog that had come by. The father glanced and said, "What a horrible-looking creature." The boy saw the dog through different eyes: "But Daddy, he wags his tail good."

Going through a rough time? Perspective can make all the difference. Someone has observed, "When it gets dark enough you can see the stars." Robert Murray McCheyne shared this advice:

"Live near to God, and all things will appear to you little in comparison with eternal realities."

When our future is foggy or fuzzy,
the Lord is our only hope.
Charles Swindoll

One hundred years from now, it won't
matter if you got that big break, or
finally traded up to a Mercedes . . . . It
will greatly matter, one hundred years
from now, that you made a
commitment to Jesus Christ.
David Shibley

Let the very worst come to pass —
even there, especially there,
His hand will hold.
Elisabeth Elliot

*Love is made complete among us so that we
will have confidence on the day of judgment.*
1 John 4:17

Intersections

There are all kinds of lines in our world. Property lines. Goal lines. Power lines. State lines. There's the bottom line, the line of fire, the scrimmage line, the base line, the skyline and the punch line. Added to those are deadlines, laugh lines, and imaginary lines. And of course, waistlines.

Think about parallel lines. Both ends of the two lines are exactly the same distance apart. If the lines could be extended into infinity, they still would be the same distance apart. But no matter how parallel they may appear, if the lines are off just a tiny, tiny bit, somewhere out in infinity those lines will come closer and closer to each other until they intersect.

Sometimes it appears that our lives are running parallel to God: that somehow we are running on different tracks, and that He is not involved in our lives.

If our lives appear to be running parallel to God, that's only an optical illusion. The spot where those two lines intersect may be at the very place we least expect it. He has arranged it so, because of His great love for us.

I am beginning to learn that it is the sweet, simple things of life which are the real ones after all.

Laura Ingalls Wilder

It is, after all, mostly little, common things that make up our lives.

Elisabeth Elliot

It isn't the great big pleasures that count the most. It's making a great deal out of the little ones.

Jean Webster

You will seek me and find me when you seek me with all your heart.
Jeremiah 29:13

Missed Free Throws

During one brief spell in the 1997-98 basketball season, the Tigers of Louisiana State University lost two close games. The team missed two free throws in the final seconds of a two-point loss at Arkansas, then missed twenty free throws against Alabama in a 60–57 loss.

Coach John Brady had this to say:

"If we make free throws at Arkansas and free throws against Alabama, we're 2–0 in the league and everybody thinks we're pretty smart."

Consider this: a free throw counts for just one point — one tiny point in a game where more than a hundred are scored by the two teams combined. Yet one missed free throw can make the difference between a loss or a victory.

In our own lives, sometimes the tiniest thing can make all the difference: a single warm smile, a handwritten note of encouragement, a warm handshake, a few moments of quiet prayer before starting the day, or a few minutes of listening to the burdens of a loved one.

Just one thing. What a difference it can make. So step to the line and give it your best shot.

All that is good, all
that is true, all that is
beautiful, all that is
beneficient, be it great
or small, be it perfect
or fragmentary,
comes from God.

John Henry Cardinal Newman

Stop and consider God's wonders.
Job 37:14

E-Mail Blessings

My daughter sends me e-mail regularly. One year a list entitled "Natural High," was making the rounds of college students around the country via e-mail. The list contained things about life the students enjoyed. At the bottom of the list, one would add his own contributions before passing it along to someone else. When my daughter sent it to me, it sparked a few ideas of my own. What were the things that I really enjoyed about life? I came up with these:

Laughing for absolutely no reason at all.

Silence.

Knowing someone will love you no matter how much you mess up.

Having enough money to help others when they really need it.

Seeing a shooting star.

Discovering a secluded waterfall, and having the time to sit and watch it for a while.

The smell of an approaching thunderstorm.

The sight of the full sun shining on the autumn colors of the trees.

The silence of snow falling at night.

Taking your time.

The rays of the sun streaming down through heavy clouds.

Working for weeks on a special surprise for someone you love, and being able to pull it off without her finding out.

Arriving home after dark on a cold night and seeing smoke rising from your chimney.

Being in love with the same person for more than twenty years.

Discovering some truth about God you didn't know before.

Getting an hour's work done before anyone gets up.

The stillness just before sunrise.

The smell of a brand-new leather Bible.

Finding something that was lost.

And I would add one more: Getting e-mail from your daughter.

Thank you, Father, for the beautiful surprises you are planning for me today.
Robert Schuller

*God's voice thunders in marvelous ways;
he does great things beyond
our understanding.*
Job 37:5

All the things in this world are gifts and signs of God's love to us. The whole world is a love letter from God.

Peter Kreeft

Let us believe that God is in all our simple deeds and learn to find him there.

A. W. Tozer

Our brightest blazes are commonly kindled by unexpected sparks.

Samuel Johnson

. . . since the creation of the world God's invisible qualities—his eternal power and divine nature—have been clearly seen, being understood from what he has made.
Romans 1:20

How can you expect God to speak in that gentle and inward voice which melts the soul, when you are making so much noise with your rapid reflections? Be silent and God will speak again.

François Fénelon

Until we take time to be quiet, we'll not hear God.

David Roper

The heart that is to be filled to the brim with holy joy must be held still.

George Seaton Bowes

Speak, Lord, for your servant is listening.
1 Samuel 3:9

Hearing God Above The Noise

The *Family Circus* comic strip once consisted of one large panel, showing a yard filled with children at play. They were blowing trumpets, honking horns, shouting, playing ball, swinging, flying kites, climbing trees, running, crying, etc.

In addition, a dog was barking, a bird was singing, and a jet was flying overhead.

Through a cutaway, one can see inside the house, where the mother says to her husband, "Listen! That's PJ crying!"

And sure enough, PJ is standing in the middle of the yard crying because one of the other children has taken his teddy bear.

There's a lot of noise in the world. Even when the world outside is quiet, there may still be a lot of noise inside our hearts and souls. Can we somehow push the noise back enough to hear the voice of God?

It sometimes takes a lot more effort than it does at other times. The key appears to be learning to filter out the din of living, long enough to hear the gentle voice of our God encouraging, lifting, soothing, challenging — and loving.

There's no other sound quite like it.

Not without design does God write the music of our lives. Be it ours to learn the time, and not be discouraged at the rests. The making of music is often a slow and painful process in this life.

John Ruskin

God manages perfectly, day and night, year in and year out, the movements of the stars, the wheeling of the planets, the staggering coordination of events that goes on the molecular level in order to hold things together. There is no doubt that He can manage the timing of my days and weeks.

Elisabeth Elliot

Those who wish to sing always find a song.

Swedish proverb

Your decrees are the theme of my song wherever I lodge.
Psalm 119:54

Listen to the Music

He watches the television commercials for upcoming motion pictures with great interest. His eyes are focused on the screen, but it's not the stars of the movie that have his attention. The storyline may be of some small interest, but even that is not what fascinates him. What enthralls him is who wrote the music for the soundtrack.

Our son Jonathan has a keen ear for such things. Many times he knows who the composer is by the way the music sounds. If he expresses an interest in seeing a movie, most often it is because he wants to hear the work of his favorite composer on the big speakers at the theater.

When we see a movie, I'm paying attention to the story. He's listening to the music. Later, when we talk about the movie, he will refer to the music which was playing at a critical moment in the plot. That's his reference point.

God has written a harmonious score for our lives that deserves to be heard. There is so much "music" in our world that it might be overlooked by those of us merely interested in the "storyline."

He's The Composer. Listen to Him.

God has revealed many truths which He
has not explained. We will just have to
be content to let Him know some things
we do not and take Him at His word.

B. A. Copass

Every problem — great or small — has
in it a treasure waiting to be discovered.

Gary and Norma Smalley

God's hand is in your heartache.
Yes, it is! If you weren't important,
do you think He would take this long
and work this hard on your life?

Charles Swindoll

*For our light and momentary troubles are
achieving for us an eternal glory
that far outweighs them all.*
2 Corinthians 4:17

Don't Waste the Suffering

Warren Wiersbe, in his book *Why Us? When Bad Things Happen to God's People,* tells of a dear friend whose husband had gone blind. The blindness was followed by an incurable disease; then the woman had a stroke which forced her to retire. They had many friends, but no children.

One day, Wiersbe writes, he attempted to encourage her by saying, "I want you to know that we're praying for you." She replied, "I appreciate that. What are you praying for God to do?"

Wiersbe writes: "When people are suffering, you pray for healing (if it's God's will), for strength, for special mercy in pain, and so on; and this is what I told her. 'Thank you,' she said, 'but please pray for one more request. Pray that I won't waste all of this suffering.' "

Wiersbe observed, "For the first time in my ministry, it struck me that our times of suffering may become times of investment, if we learn how to pray about them."

The lesson? Be sure that, regardless of what you may be going through, *the suffering is not wasted!*

Amazing, isn't it, that our prayers,
whether grand and glorious or feeble
and faint, can move the very heart of
God who created the universe?

Joni Eareckson Tada

Sometimes God delays the answer to
our prayer in final form until we have
time to build up the strength, accumu-
late the knowledge, or fashion the character that would make it possible for
him to say yes to what we ask.

Samuel Pepys

God warms His hands
at our hearts when we pray

Unknown

*We do not know what we ought to pray, but
the Spirit himself intercedes for us with
groans that words cannot express.*
Romans 8:26

Abba Dabba Ahmin

In a comic strip, a little baby is sitting in her high chair, her hands folded in front of her, an angelic expression on her face. She is saying, "Abba Dabba Ahmin!"

Her parents are looking around the corner, and her mother says, "Look — she's trying to say the blessing." The little girl takes a taste from the bowl in front of her, then prays again — this time more forcefully: "Abba Dabba AHMIN!"

The final frame of the strip shows the little girl making a face after taking another taste. She is thinking, "STILL tastes like mush!"

Sadly, that's the way many of us approach prayer. We expect God to change hot dogs into steak, F's into A's, or bankruptcy into wealth — just because we utter some magic words.

Prayer is not a quick fix, as much as it is a piece of our fellowship and relationship with God. Yes, sometimes He does work miracles, and we're all glad that He does!

However, much of the time God deliberately chooses NOT to answer our prayers the way we want, because He has something far, far better to give us. AHMIN!

Cripple him, and you have
a Sir Walter Scott.
Lock him in a prison cell, and
you have a John Bunyan.
Bury him in the snows of Valley Forge,
and you have a George Washington.
Afflict him with asthma as a child,
and you have a Theodore Roosevelt.
Make him play second fiddle in an
obscure South American orchestra,
and you have a Toscanini.
Deny her the ability to see, hear, and
speak, and you have a Helen Keller.

Abigail Van Buren

*Always give yourselves fully to the work of
the Lord, because you know that your labor
in the Lord is not in vain.*
1 Corinthians 15:58b

The Vine in the Maze

The Continental Oil Company once had a full-page advertisement in a national magazine. The ad consisted mainly of a drawing of a vine trapped inside a maze. The vine had sent out one shoot after another, trying to find the light of the sun, only to reach a dead end every time.

Finally, there was one shoot which wound its way around corners and through the maze until it reached the only exit. In the freedom it reached upward toward the sunshine.

The point was that the company was constantly searching for alternative sources of energy. The headline in the ad read: "Nature doesn't explore just one path to reach a goal. Neither should man."

Let's apply those words in as many ways as we can to our own lives. It is inevitable that we will run up against obstacles from time to time. When we're reached a dead-end, do we give up, or do we keep trying?

> *. . . let us run with perseverance*
> *the race marked out for us.*
> Hebrews 12:1b

Send me anywhere,
only go with me.
Lay any burden on me,
only sustain me.
Sever any tie that binds
but the tie that binds
me to Thy service
and to Thy heart.

David Livingstone

*If anyone serves, he should do it with
the strength God provides.*
1 Peter 4:11

Milking Reindeer

A couple became interested in helping a Finnish girl migrate to the U. S. They decided she might be a good prospect for a job in their home.

They questioned her qualifications: Could she cook? Do housework? Could she take care of young children? No: her mother did the cooking, sister did the housework, and grandmother took care of the younger children.

So, finally, they asked, "What would you do if you worked for us?" "Well," said the girl, "I could milk reindeer."

In our world, there are too many of us who want to milk reindeer when there are no reindeer which need milking. Instead, there's a young girl who needs a big sister or a mother-figure. There's a family who could use an extra bag of groceries on their doorstep tonight. There's a young man who has great potential for God's Kingdom, but right now just needs someone to believe in him.

Not too many reindeer are waiting to be milked. Find the *real* jobs — and do them.

We need to recapture the power of imagination; we shall find that life can be full of wonder, mystery, beauty and joy.

Sir Harold Spencer Jones

If you are seeking creative ideas, go out walking. Angels whisper to a man when he goes for a walk.

Raymond Inman

Sometimes Jesus is our strength simply to sit still . . . the answers will come.

Billy Graham

Show the wonders of your great love. . . .
Psalm 17:7

Kick Back

Do you feel guilty if you allow yourself a few minutes' luxury of daydreaming? There's always something to do, isn't there? Paul MacCready once stated in a speech:

"The only ideas I've ever had have come from daydreaming, but modern life keeps people from daydreaming. Every moment of the day your mind is being occupied, controlled, by someone else — at school, at work, watching television. . . . You need to just kick back in a chair and let your mind daydream."

Schedule it on your calendar if you have to, but carve out some time when you can put your feet up and stare out the window. Take an hour and go sit quietly under a tree, with no book, no companion and no agenda.

One important idea that might come to you while there is that there is nothing you face which is bigger or more powerful than our God.

So go ahead. Kick back and try to imagine anything — *anything* — bigger than God. Then strengthen yourself with the image of God wrapped around you.

What comfort!

"For I know the plans I have for you," declares the Lord, *"plans to prosper you and not to harm you, plans to give you hope and a future."*

Jeremiah 29:11

When He Doesn't
Do It Your Way

Do you remember the story of the Old Testament prophet Elijah, hiding from Queen Jezebel? He was cowering in a cave when he heard God's voice; "What are you doing here, Elijah?"

The story is found in 1 Kings 19:9-18. God told Elijah to go stand out on the mountain. A series of amazing things happened. First, there was a powerful wind that tore the mountain apart. That was followed by an earthquake, then a fire. The Bible says that God was not in the wind, the earthquake or the fire.

God does not always work in the manner we think He should. The Scripture tells us that after the fire, there was a "still small voice," or as some translations put it, "a gentle whisper."

With great insight into our human natures, Arthur DeKruyter has written, "If we had been with Elijah in the cave, waiting for God to speak, we probably would have rushed into the earthquake and tossed around a few rocks ourselves. We would have huffed and puffed along with the windstorm God sent. We would have been so busy talking about things that we probably wouldn't even have heard the still, small voice when He did speak!"

When God doesn't do things our way, we have several options:

One, we can blame Him for not paying attention to what is really going on in our lives.

Two, we can question His love for us, telling ourselves that He is too big and impersonal to care about us.

Three, we can ignore the whole situation, and convince ourselves that it will go away in time.

Or four, we can believe that our Heavenly Father loves His children far too much to ignore our pleas for help.

By far, the fourth option is the best. Because His ways are higher than our ways, He doesn't always do things the way we think He should. Our ideas are too narrow, our vision too limited and our imaginations too cramped to fully comprehend the wondrous ways of God.

In the meantime, just *trust Him.*

The Almighty does nothing without reason, though the frail mind of man cannot explain the reason.

St. Augustine

There is no circumstance, no trouble,
no testing, that can ever touch me until,
first of all, it has gone past God
and past Christ, right through to me.
If it has come that far, it has come
with a great purpose, which I may not
understand at the moment.
But I refuse to become panicky,
as I lift up my eyes to him and accept it
as coming from the throne of God
for some great purpose of blessing
to my own heart.

Alan Redpath

The Lord is good to those whose hope is in
him, to the one who seeks him.
Lamentations 3:25

Men go abroad to wonder at the heights of mountains, at the huge waves of the sea, at the long courses of the rivers, at the vast compass of the ocean; at the circular motions of the stars; and they pass by themselves without wondering.

St. Augustine

Our Creator would never have made such lovely days and given us the deep hearts to enjoy them, above and beyond all thoughts, unless we were meant to be immortal.

Nathaniel Hawthorne

For the scientist who has lived by his faith in the power of reason, the story ends like a bad dream. He has scaled the mountains of ignorance; he is about to conquer the highest peak; as he pulls himself over the final rock, he is greeted by a band of theologians who have been sitting there for centuries.

Robert Jastrow

Watermelon Seeds

Sometimes the smallest thing can teach us the biggest lessons. Take watermelon seeds. William Jennings Bryan was intrigued by them. He mused:

"I have observed the power of the watermelon seed. It has the power of drawing from the ground and through itself 200,000 times its weight. When you can tell me how it takes this material and out of it colors an outside surface beyond the imitation of art, and then forms inside of it a white rind and within that again a red heart, thickly inlaid with black seeds, each one of which in turn is capable of drawing through itself 200,000 times its weight — when you can explain to me the mystery of a watermelon, you can ask me to explain the mystery of God."

While taking care of tasks that are really important, we should not overlook the little things that brush up against our souls every day.

It might be a watermelon seed, or an ant, or brief eye contact with a total stranger, or any of a thousand things we could name. Each of them has its own message from God, all of them sounding like this: *"This is God. I love you."*

When you get into a tight place,
and everything goes against you,
till it seems as though you could not
hang on a minute longer, never
give up then, for that is just the place
and time that the tide will turn.
Harriet Beecher Stowe

Character consists in what you do
on the third and fourth tries.
James Michener

God always answers in the deeps, never
in the shallows of our souls.
Amy Carmichael

*. . . in all these things we are more than
conquerors through him who loved us.*
Romans 8:37

Conquering Your
Personal Jericho

The Old Testament book of Joshua is a fascinating story. God led the Hebrew people from four decades of wandering around in the desert, to begin the process of receiving wonderful blessings in the land of Canaan.

There were two immediate obstacles. One, they would have to cross the Jordan River, but it was at flood stage. Two, the fortified city of Jericho stood just a short distance away on the other side.

If you have not already, one day you will find yourself in the position of not knowing where to turn, or what to do. You are up against your own personal Jericho. God says to go forward, and you would like very much to do just that. But just in front of you appears to be an inconquerable stronghold. The situation looks impossible.

What does your "Jericho" look like? It could be a monumental challenge which is much, much bigger than you are. It could be a temptation of some sort. It could be a recurring problem with depression. It might be a health crisis in your life or in the life of someone you love. Your Jericho may take the form of a broken relationship, or money problems, or difficulty in being accepted by other people.

But we all have them. Let us remember that sometimes God sends us through the wilderness and through the river, and tells us to do what appears to be impossible. He does this just so we can learn to depend on Him and on Him alone for all He commands.

The crashing wave finally reaches peace as it breaks upon the land. . . . so our turbulent spirits find rest, as we break upon the vast shoreline of God's love.

Janet Weaver

Be strong and courageous, and do the work.
1 Chronicles 28:20

The beauty remains; the pain passes.
Auguste Renoir
(when asked why he continued
to paint while suffering from arthritis)

We sometimes fear to bring our troubles
to God, because they must seem so
small to Him who sitteth on the circle on
the earth. But if they are large enough to
vex and endanger our welfare, they are
large enough to touch His heart of love.
R. A. Torrey

God will never let you be shaken or
moved from your place near His heart.
Joni Eareckson Tada

Everything is possible for him who believes.
Mark 9:23

The fierce grip of panic
need not immobilize you.
God knows no limitation
when it comes to deliverance.
Admit your fear.
Commit it to Him.
Dump the pressure on Him.
He can handle it.

Charles R. Swindoll

*The eternal God is your refuge, and
underneath are the everlasting arms.*
Deuteronomy 33:27

It Can't Be Done

Many years ago, "experts" in Germany believed that if trains moved at the frightful speed of 15 miles an hour, blood would spurt from the travelers' noses. Passengers would suffocate when moving through tunnels.

In 1881, when the New York YMCA announced typing lessons for women, vigorous protests were made. It was believed that the female constitution would break down under the strain.

Joshua Coppersmith was once arrested in Boston for trying to sell stock in a telephone company. He was told, "All well-informed people know that it is impossible to transmit the human voice over a wire."

"I can't do that." We may have programmed ourselves into believing that the situation is too difficult. Finding the strength to face another day, to smile in the fog of living, or to be excited about life in general may seem impossible.

But find something that God can't handle. Now *that's* something that can't be done.

The God who
orchestrates the
universe has a good
many things to
consider that have
not occurred to me,
and it is well that I
leave them to Him.

Elisabeth Elliot

I know that you can do all things;
no plan of yours can be thwarted.
Job 42:2

Saddle Up

It can be a very frightening experience for a wild horse to feel a saddle on its back for the first time. Some horses react with anger. They rear back and kick and struggle to get away. Nostrils flare, eyeballs roll back and panic takes over.

Other horses are so afraid they cannot move. They just stand in one spot as though frozen, shaking and trembling like a leaf on a tree.

When something unpleasant happens, do you react with anger, lashing out at other people, even at God? Perhaps something has occurred which you cannot control or change, and you're so angry about it that you are determined someone is going to pay for your discomfort. Or maybe the fear has immobilized you. You're afraid to step one way or the other, thinking that if you do you'll make a fatal mistake.

The growing Christian can be compared to a horse which has learned to trust its trainer. The maturing Christian has grown over time to learn what the saddle is for. He knows that when the saddle of trouble and difficulty is suddenly thrust upon him, it is there for a purpose — a purpose of greater love than we can imagine.

Each of us may be sure that if God sends us on stony paths, He will provide us with strong shoes, and He will not send us out on any journey for which He does not equip us well.

Alexander Maclaren

Do not let Satan deceive you into being afraid of God's plans for your life.

R. A. Torrey

God is never at a loss to know what He's going to do in our situations. He knows perfectly well what is best for us. Our problem is, we don't know.

Charles Swindoll

Who of you by worrying can add a single hour to his life?
Matthew 6:27

Choking Out Worry

To the Greeks, worry was something which tears a man in two, dragging him in opposite directions. Their word for "worry" described a garment coming apart at the seams.

The Anglo-Saxon word described a power gripping a man by the throat, as a wolf seizes a sheep and strangles all the vitality out of it.

Our English word is actually related to words such as "wreath," "wrinkle," "wrong," and "wrist." The idea behind every one of these words is that of something twisted: a wreath is made up of materials twisted or wound up in a circle; a wrinkle originally conveyed the idea of something which had been twisted; if something is wrong, it is because the truth has become twisted; and a wrist is a joint which can be bent and twisted.

So worry is something which twists, or strangles, the neck or spirit. Someone has pointed out that worry, if left unchecked, soon can choke the "abundant" out of life.

Instead, choke out worry by remembering that your Heavenly Father can handle it. Whatever "it" may happen to be.

If we had no winter,
the spring would not
be so pleasant;
if we did not sometimes
taste of adversity,
prosperity would not
be so welcome.

Anne Bradstreet

*See! The winter is past; the rains are over
and gone. Flowers appear on the earth;
the season of singing has come.*
Song of Songs 2:11-12

Springtime

When you see the word "summer" what images pop into your mind? Your answer might range from the end of the school year to swimming to hot weather to baseball to vacations to farming to picnics.

"Autumn" conjures up mental pictures of cooler weather, crisp apples, the colors in trees, going back to school, the harvest, Thanksgiving and football games.

"Winter" may cause you to think of Christmas, New Year's, frost, snow, roaring fireplaces, bare trees, family gatherings or basketball.

But what is your first thought when you hear the word "spring"? Do you think of the breezes that come in March or the rains that come in April? Do you think of the tender shoots of grass, the returning birds, or the fragile little flowers that bloom? It may be Easter or the Resurrection, or spring break and the approaching end of the school year.

Spiritually speaking, which of the seasons would you use to describe your relationship with God right now? Perhaps you are feeling or have felt that period in your life which could be described as "winter," when your very soul seems to have been frozen in suspended animation. Perhaps your relationship with God is stale and flat; your spirit is suffocating from want of a breath of fresh air from God; your heart feels restricted and confined.

David did not use the seasons to represent his walk with God, but he did use a rather unique expression to describe what God had done for him: "You have set my heart free!" (Psalm 119:32).

God can set your heart free! He can give you a spiritual springtime, a renewal of your spirit, a rejuvenation of your relationship to Him. Your soul can open up and blossom under the warmth of His love.

And it can happen today.

There is something in every season,
in every day, to celebrate
with thanksgiving.
Gloria Gaither

Your promise renews my life.
Psalm 119:50b

Winter has an uncanny way of
producing in us a great appreciation
for the tender new beginnings
of spring . . . both in nature
and in our hearts.

Janet Weaver

When we focus on God, the scene
changes. He's in control of our lives;
nothing lies outside the realm of
his redemptive grace. Even when
we make mistakes, fail in relationships,
or deliberately make bad choices,
God can redeem us.

Penelope J. Stokes

*Your word is a lamp to my feet
and a light for my path.*
Psalm 119:105

There is no greener pasture than where
the Shepherd leads you.

Jan Carlberg

It is in silence that God is known,
and through mysteries that
he declares himself.

Robert H. Benson

The best qualities of our spiritual
lives are matured by quietness,
silence and commonplace.

A. P. Gouthey

A solitude is the
audience-chamber of God.

Walter Savage Landor

*Devote yourselves to prayer,
being watchful and thankful.*
Colossians 4:2

Solitude

Josh Billings called it "a good place to visit, but a poor place to stay." Jean de La Bruyere stated that it was a "great misfortune . . . to be incapable of solitude." Carl Sandburg figured that we have not cultivated the habit of solitude because we are afraid of being alone:

"Shakespeare, Leonardo da Vinci, Benjamin Franklin, and Lincoln never saw a movie, heard a radio, or looked at a TV. They had 'loneliness' and knew what to do with it. They were not afraid of being lonely because they knew that was when the creative mood in them would mark."

Dietrich Bonhoeffer sensed a certain value of solitude when he wrote, "It is as though in solitude the soul develops senses which we hardly know in everyday life."

It is important to understand that there is a vast difference between being lonely and being alone. It is also important to distinguish between being alone with God in solitude, and merely being alone.

The man or woman of God thrives on the times when he or she can be alone with God, just being still and quiet before Him.

We often reject a passing good that
God offers us because we want
or expect some other good.
Terry Lindvall

There is nothing that makes us love
a man so much as praying for him.
William Law

The way to love someone is to lightly
run your finger over that person's soul
until you find a crack, and then gently
pour your love into that crack.
Keith Miller

*Bear with each other and forgive whatever
grievance you may have against one another.*
Colossians 3:13

Jumping to Conclusions

Someone observed once that the only exercise some people get is jumping to conclusions.

It was said that the English pulpiteer Charles Spurgeon and his wife owned several chickens. They refused to give any of the eggs away to friends, even telling relatives that they could have any eggs they paid for.

Many people decided that the couple was greedy. The Spurgeons endured the criticisms for years without offering any defense or explanation. It was only years later, after Mrs. Spurgeon died, that the whole story became known.

It seems that the couple been using the profits from the sale of the eggs to help support two elderly widows.

Things are not always what they seem. We might do ourselves and others a great favor if we could avoid arriving at conclusions prematurely.

Jumping to conclusions isn't a very healthy activity at all.

Try patience, kindness, understanding and faith instead. They could use a little exercise.

God has a thousand ways
Where I cannot see one;
When all my means have
reached their end
Then His have just begun.

Esther Guyot

All that we have and are is one of the
unique and never-to-be-repeated
ways God has chosen to express
Himself in space and time.

Brennan Manning

Even when we cannot see the why and
wherefore of God's dealings, we know
that there is love in and behind them,
and so we can rejoice always.

J. I. Packer

Find rest, O my soul, in God alone.
Psalm 62:5

Things Are Not Always What They Seem

In 1941, star halfback Johnny Chung was leading his football team to a storybook season. Plainfield Teachers College won its first four games by scores of 13-0, 27-0, 35-0 and 23-0.

The *New York Times* reported that Chung had scored 57 of his team's 98 points in those four games, averaging a gain of 9.3 yards every time he touched the football.

Then suddenly, after winning a fifth game, Plainfield suddenly stopped playing. The *Times* reported that the team had disbanded, due to many of the players failing mid-term examinations.

But things are not always what they seem. The truth was that the whole story was a hoax. Plainfield Teachers College never existed, nor did any of the schools it had supposedly beaten. A stockbroker on Wall Street dreamed up the whole thing.

But here is something that wasn't just dreamed up:

". . . for you, Lord, have never forsaken those who seek you" (Psalm 9:10).

Every morning is a fresh beginning.
Every day the world is made new.
Today is a new day. Today is my world
made new. I have lived all my life up to
this moment, to come to this day.
This moment — this day — is as good as
any moment in all eternity.
I shall make of this day — each moment
of this day — a heaven on earth. This
is my day of opportunity.

Dan Custer

Each day of our lives we make deposits
in the memory banks of our children.
Charles R. Swindoll

Make the most of every opportunity.
Colossians 4:5b

What's Really Important?

Michael J. Fox, television and movie star, is the father of three children. His successes are not the most important things to him, however.

Fox has said, "I know what it's like to have a $200 million movie. I know what it's like to eat with the Queen of England. And it doesn't mean as much as sitting on the floor today with my kids."

Someone has noted that "time, like a snowflake, disappears while we're trying to decide what to do with it." You can hang on to every second and every precious moment with all your might, but suddenly, they are gone.

We have only one life to experience here on earth. Make sure that you focus on the things that really matter. Meeting that deadline at work could be the most important thing, but it might be sitting on the floor playing with your kids instead. The housework can wait; the lawn can be mowed tomorrow.

But the opportunity to experience life — real life — is here now.

So, go sit on the floor with your kids.

It's okay.

You may be sorry that you spoke,
Sorry you stayed or went,
Sorry you won or lost,
Perhaps, sorry so much was spent.
But as you go through life, you'll find
You're never sorry you were kind.

Unknown

All the beautiful sentiments in the world
weigh less than a single lovely action.

Unknown

*. . . clothe yourselves with compassion,
kindness, humility, gentless and patience.*
Colossians 3:12b

Guilty of Kindness

Sylvia Stayton was once arrested for being kind. No, really. She was brought to trial and fined $500 — for putting money in other people's expired parking meters.

Before arresting her, an officer had warned the 63-year-old grandmother of 10 that she was guilty of breaking an obscure city ordinance.

Sylvia quickly became a local folk hero in the Cincinnati area. To help with her legal defense fund, one group printed up T-shirts that read, "Sylvia Stayton . . . guilty of kindness."

It may not have been as dramatic as that, but have you ever been accused of kindness? Was there enough evidence to convict?

In the day in front of you, can you think of some opportunity which might allow you to demonstrate an unusual degree of kindness toward someone else? Will you help someone who cannot help themselves? Will you be Christ-like toward someone who is doing his best to make your day difficult?

Decide now you will be guilty of "premeditated kindness."

One thing we may be sure of, however:
For the believer all pain has meaning;
all adversity is profitable. There is no
question that adversity is difficult. It
usually takes us by surprise and seems
to strike where we are most vulnerable.
To us it often appears completely
senseless and irrational, but to God
none of it is either senseless
or irrational. He has a purpose in
every pain He brings or allows in
our lives. We can be sure that in
some way He intends it for our
profit and His glory.

Jerry Bridges

Create in me a pure heart, O God, and
renew a steadfast spirit within me.
Psalm 51:10

Adjustments

Occasionally, scientists add one additional second to their atomic clocks, making that particular month one-sixtieth of a second longer. Atomic clocks run independently of the rotation of the Earth, and occasionally they have to be adjusted. Our planet's rotation at times speeds up and sometimes slows down — something scientists haven't yet been able to understand.

Why is it important that one tiny second be added to the world's clocks? In our day, exact time is needed for modern navigation, among other things.

Ships and aircraft use satellite signals and radio waves to help determine their location. An error as tiny as a millionth of a second can produce a position error of a quarter mile. That may not matter much when a ship is in the middle of the ocean, but it's not a very good thing to happen whenever a pilot is attempting to land a jumbo jet on a runway in a metropolitan area.

So, to keep everything running the way they should, an adjustment has to be made to the atomic clocks.

How many adjustments have you made to

your life in Christ lately? At times our spiritual growth races at an accelerated speed, while at other times it merely crawls or halts altogether. It serves us well to stop periodically to examine ourselves before God and make any adjustments which appear to be necessary.

A daily quiet time before God can alert us to subtle changes in our love for and commitment to Christ. Considering our very human tendency to fall short, the necessity of such a time of examination increases with the passing of time.

There is only one relationship that matters, and that is your personal relationship to a personal Redeemer and Lord. Let everything else go, but maintain that at all costs, and God will fulfill His purpose through your life.
Oswald Chambers

Blessed is he whose transgressions are forgiven, whose sins are covered.
Psalm 32:1

God is for us far more, at times, than we would prefer. He is committed to removing all vestiges of sin from our souls when we wish He'd be satisfied with a clean new outfit. His interest in us far exceeds our concerns. Our perspective is usually limited to achieving a better life, and His desire for us is radical conformity to His Son's perfect character. No wonder He seems like an enemy when His discipline begins to grind off our arrogance in order to perfect His beauty.

Dan B. Allender

Godly sorrow brings repentance that leads to salvation.
2 Corinthians 7:10

Opportunity doesn't necessarily knock on the door; it may be leaning against the wall waiting to be noticed.

Unknown

Recognize your responsibilities and you will see your opportunities.

William Arthur Ward

. . . love one another deeply, from the heart. . .
1 Peter 1:22b

It Isn't Too Late

"If you can do something that turns out wrong, you can almost always put it right, get over it, learn from it, or at least deny it. But once you've missed out on something, it's gone. There will be the girl you never got to say the right words to, the band you never got to see live, the winning streak you never go to cheer on, the brilliant retiring professor whose class you never took, the relative you never got very close with. It's a long list no matter what. Try to keep it as short as possible."

Gordon Drizschilo

What about the opportunity to write that letter of encouragement we've been intending? The phone call? The visit?

What about that neighbor who needs a friend?

What about that book or song you've been meaning to write?

The child you've intended to hug?

The spouse or parent who needs to hear the words "I love you" come from your lips?

A man with two watches is never quite sure what time it is.

Unknown

But one thing I do: Forgetting what is behind and straining toward what is ahead I press on toward the goal to win the prize for which God has called me heavenward in Christ Jesus.
Philippians 3:13

Choose One Chair

Although the sun bombards the earth every hour with billions of kilowatts of energy, we can protect ourselves from most of its effects with a hat and sunscreen. On the other hand a laser can take just a few watts of energy, focus them in a coherent stream of light and drill a hole through a diamond.

The difference is *focus*. Tenor superstar Luciano Pavarotti learned the importance of focus from his father. The young Luciano became a pupil of a professional tenor in his hometown of Modena, Italy. At the same time, he enrolled in a teachers' college.

When he graduated, Luciano asked his father, "Shall I be a teacher or a singer?"

His father replied, "Luciano, if you try to sit on two chairs, you will fall between them. For life, you must choose one chair."

The now-famous tenor wrote years later: "I think whether it's laying bricks, writing a book — whatever we choose — we should give ourselves to it. Commitment, that's the key. Choose one chair."

Focus!

I believe that even our mistakes
and shortcomings are turned to good
account, and that is no harder for
God to deal with them than with
our supposedly good deeds.

Dietrich Bonhoeffer

He who never made a mistake
never made a discovery.

Samuel Smiles

Failure is success if we learn from it.

Malcolm Forbes

May your unfailing love be my comfort.
Psalm 119:76

Really Dumb

A man walked into a convenience store, put a $20 bill on the counter and asked for change. When the clerk opened the cash drawer, the man pulled a gun and asked for all the cash in the register, which the clerk promptly provided. The man took the cash from the clerk and fled — leaving the $20 bill on the counter. The total amount of cash he got from the drawer? Fifteen dollars.

Another man entered a drug store, flashed a gun, announced a robbery, and pulled a Hefty-bag face mask over his head — then realized that he'd forgotten to cut eyeholes in the mask.

We may never have tried to rob anyone, but chances are very likely that, given the fact that we are human, we have done something dumb — really, really dumb.

The embarrassment sticks with us for a long time. It's a great thing to know that our Heavenly Father doesn't laugh at us when we make mistakes. He's far more interested in making sure that even our really dumb misdeeds can be turned into something good.

Not learning from our mistakes — now that's *really* dumb.

God's purposes are often hidden from us. He owes us no explanations. We owe Him our complete love and trust.
Warren Wiersbe

Faith goes up the stairs that love has made and looks out of the windows which hope has opened.
Charles Haddon Spurgeon

There is no conceivable situation in which it is not safe to trust God.
J. Oswald Sanders

You are my hiding place.
Psalm 32:7

Plum-Tree Faith

In her book, *North to the Orient,* Anne Morrow Lindbergh speaks of the oriental symbolism of trees. The bamboo stands for prosperity. The pine tree means long life. The plum tree suggests courage. Mrs. Lindbergh had asked a friend why the plum tree stood for courage. The answer was, "because it puts out its blossoms while the snow is still on the ground."

Some trees stand straight and tall, while others are twisted and bent. Many times we Christians won't move ahead until we are absolutely sure it is "safe."

Perhaps we need to pray that God would give us a "Plum Tree Faith." You know, the kind of faith that blossoms in the face of circumstances that appear bleak and discouraging — a courageous faith.

So when the snow is falling in your life, ask God to give you an extra measure of courage. Just on the other side of the winter is a beautiful Spring.

And few things are any better than a juicy plum in early Spring. You know what I mean.

Faith is what binds us to Christ when everything is gone, including our most cherished expectations of him.

M. Craig Barnes

Every day is a messenger of God.

Russian proverb

Earth, with her thousand voices, praises God.

Samuel Taylor Coleridge

For we are God's workmanship, created in Christ Jesus to do good works, which God prepared in advance for us to do.
Ephesians 2:10

No Lemon for the Fish

A British columnist once wrote about the complaints of two music critics. He commented: "If this pair had been present at the miracle of the loaves and fishes, one of them would have complained that there was no lemon to go with the fish, and the other would have demanded more butter for the bread."

It's true. When Jesus performed this miracle, He did not provide either lemon or butter — yet it was just as powerful a miracle. Just ask those who were there that day.

The lesson is that sometimes God works miracles in our lives by giving us the bare necessities, just enough and no more.

He knows what we need. There is nothing beyond His capability to provide. It's just that — and this is something difficult to understand — there are times that God withholds the lemon so we will trust Him that much more.

God lavishes His abundance on us, even if we are not always grateful. He provides the fish, and sometimes He tosses a little lemon in with it. If He chooses not to include the extras, however, let us be grateful for what He *does* give.

Christians are not citizens of earth
trying to get to heaven but citizens
of heaven making their way
through this world.

Vance Havner

Trust with a childlike dependence on
God, and no trouble can destroy you.

Billy Graham

We talk about gates of pearl and
streets of gold and walls of jasper,
and we are thrilled; but those things
would not be attractive if Jesus were
not there. His presense is what will
make heaven such a grand place.

Paul Rees

*. . . we have a building from God, an eternal
house in heaven, not built by human hands.*
2 Corinthians 5:1

Out of This World

It was an exciting time! In 1997, the United States' spacecraft Pathfinder landed on Mars. People around the world were watching. We marveled at the technology which would enable humans to complete such an amazing task.

But not everyone was thrilled. Two men in Yemen filed a lawsuit against NASA in a Yemeni court, claiming that the United States was trespassing. They claimed the planet was left to them by ancestors 3,000 years ago.

We don't know about that. But we do know that the followers of Jesus Christ can claim a much greater inheritance. Unlike the claim of the Yemeni pair, believers in Christ actually have a claim to the riches in glory in Christ Jesus.

This is the way the Apostle Paul described it: "Now if we are children, then we are heirs— heirs of God and co-heirs with Christ . . . ." (Romans 8:17a). "And my God will meet all your needs according to his glorious riches in Christ Jesus" (Philippians 4:19)

Mars? They can have it. We have Heaven! And it's out of this world.

If I obey Jesus Christ in the seemingly random circumstances of life, they become pinholes through which I see the face of God.

Oswald Chambers

There is nothing quite as exhilarating as getting out of bed in the morning, going back into the world, and knowing why. It is thrilling knowledge that I am fulfilling God's intended purpose for me.

Bill Hull

How do I love God? By doing beautifully the work I have been given to do, by doing simply that which God has entrusted to me, in whatever form it takes.

Mother Teresa

Each one should use whatever gift he has received to serve others, faithfully administering God's grace in its various forms.
1 Peter 4:10

Walnuts in the Attic

A young boy left his log-cabin home in the mountains and went off to explore life. Thirty-five years later, he returned to the old home place, now abandoned. While there, he remembered that as a young boy he had brought a bag of walnuts to the old milk house by the spring.

Twenty-five of those walnuts he had planted along the creek bed, and now there stood a row of beautiful walnut trees.

On the same day, he had taken what was left of the bag of walnuts and left them in the attic of the milk house. Searching for them, he found the bag under a heavy layer of dust.

Those which had been planted grew into strong and healthy trees, but the others had long before become useless.

Do you have any walnuts in your attic? Any talent you have hidden? Pull them out, blow the dust off, and plant them. Watch what comes up.

Never be lacking in zeal, but keep your spiritual fervor, serving the Lord.
Romans 12:1

Sometimes being pushed to the
wall gives you the momentum
necessary to get over it!

Peter de Jager

Did you know that the things
which are happening to you right
now are to prepare you to fulfill
a beautiful dream that God wants
to place in your life?

Dale E. Galloway

Give to us clear vision that we may
know where to stand and what to
stand for. Let us not be content to
wait and see what will happen, but
give us the determination to make
the right things happen.

Peter Marshall

Prepare your minds for action.
1 Peter 1:13

Throwing Your Cap
Over the Wall

Former President John Kennedy liked to tell about his grandfather, Fitzgerald. As a small boy in Ireland, Fitzgerald would walk home from school with a group of boys. The others in the group would climb over the jagged, high cobblestone walls near the path home, since that route would be shorter.

Some of the fences were 10-12 feet high, and were difficult to climb. But one day, Fitzgerald took his cap off and threw it over the wall. Going home without his cap meant that he would be punished, so he knew he would have to climb over to retrieve it. And he did.

Each of us occasionally needs to create a challenge for ourselves, which forces us to reach out farther than normal, to do something we would not normally do.

Isn't that what faith is about? What walls are crowding your life, perhaps blocking your way? They loom over you, intimidating you and draining your enthusiasm. Perhaps it's time to throw your cap over a wall.

But be sure to go after it!

Let your faith in Christ be in the quiet confidence that He will every day and every moment keep you as the apple of His eye, keep you in perfect peace and in the sure experience of all the light and the strength you need.

Andrew Murray

Somewhere on the great world the sun is always shining, and just so sure as you live, it will sometime shine on you. The dear God made it so. There is so much sunshine we must all have our share.

Myrtle Reed

Be at rest once more, O my soul,
for the Lord has been good to you.
Psalm 116:7

Behind the Clouds

Ever flown in a jet on a cloudy day? As the plane rose above the clouds, you were able to see the sun was indeed shining brightly.

Oswald Chambers, in *Run Today's Race*, wrote: "Why does God bring thunderclouds and disasters when we want green pastures and still waters? Bit by bit we find behind the clouds, the Father's feet; behind the lightning, an abiding day that has no night; behind the thunder, 'a still, small voice' that comforts with a comfort that is unspeakable."

In *Reflections on Nature,* Phillip Keller observed, "For all of us life comes with sunshine and storm, the passing years bear to us their clamour and their calm. Out of the tangled threads of our days our Father quietly weaves a tapestry of beauty and quiet contentment, if we let Him. A golden glow lingers after the gale. There is stillness in which to whisper, "Oh Christ, You are here!"

There are a lot of clouds and storms in our lives, aren't there? Learn to look past them to see "our Father's feet," and the "golden glow" of Christ's presence. It really makes a difference.

To be grateful is to recognize the love
of God in everything He has given us —
and He has given us everything.
Every breath we draw is a gift of
His love, every moment of
existence a gift of grace.

Thomas Merton

Something to be thankful for is that
you're here to be thankful.

Barbara Johnson

Seeing our Father in everything makes
life one long thanksgiving and gives a
rest of heart.

Hannah Whitall Smith

*Give thanks in all circumstances, for this
is God's will for you in Christ Jesus.*
1 Thessalonians 5:18

Tat You

When our daughter, Jennifer, now a young woman, was just a toddler and barely talking, she taught me a lot about faith.

She had one of those little cups with a lid on it, so very little would spill out if she dropped it or knocked it over. Her mother and I were trying to get her to say "Please" and "Thank You," but she was still having trouble remembering which was which.

So she had developed a habit of coming up to us, holding out her little cup to be refilled, and saying, "Tat you."

She fully expected her mom or dad to fill her cup, and so she was saying, "thank you" in advance. How often have I gone to my Heavenly Father, held out my cup and said, "Thank You" even before the answer was in sight?

*How can I repay the Lord
for all his goodness to me?*
Psalm 116:12

Spring is God thinking in gold,
laughing in blue, and
speaking in green.

Frank Johnson

One of *summer's* best fragrances is
neither fruit nor flower; it is the smell of
rain when the first drops come down
and sink into the grateful hot earth or
onto hot, dry stones. If peace has a
fragrance, it is the fragrance of this rain.

Rachel Peden

Autumn paints a subtle sermon
without benefit of words.

Thelma Ireland

Winter has a mood and mystery
all her own. She has learned from her
Creator that everything needs a time to
rest and recharge for the glories
that lie just ahead.

Rocky Henriques

What's It For?

Shirley Bartko once wrote in *Reader's Digest* that she and her family had always lived in warm climates. Her little boy had never seen snow. Soon after they moved to Pennsylvania, the area received the first snow of the season.

The next morning, Shirley and her little boy, Billy, stood at the picture window, looking at the beauty. Billy was quiet for a long time, then asked, "What's it for, Mom?"

That's a very good question. Have you considered that lately? What is it really for, anyway? Why did God create such a thing as snow? Or spring? Or autumn? Or lightning?

Come to think of it, God could have created the world in black and white, but He added color. If God would do such wonderful things in such marvelous, minute detail, should it surprise any of us that He loved the world so much that He sent His One and Only Son?

Should we be surprised that He loves us so much that He chooses to become involved in our lives, providing hope and guidance when we had none?

So what's it for? It's for *love.*

God is always working just beyond our limits, inviting us to venture into the unknown where we are abandoned by everything — especially by our prior expectations of God.

M. Craig Barnes

God has a time for everything, a perfect schedule. He is never too soon, never too late. The when of His will is as important as the what and the how.

Richard C. Halverson

Faith enables the believing soul to treat the future as present and the invisible as seen.

J. Oswald Sanders

Make level paths for your feet and take only ways that are firm
Proverbs 4:26

Catching the Knife
by the Handle

An old Oriental proverb gives us an interesting perspective: "If life throws a knife at you, there are two ways of catching it — by the blade and by the handle."

Most certainly, life throws knives at us. Many are the days when we feel as though we had a bright target painted in flaming red on our backs. What makes the difference is how we react to the grief and disappointment which comes our way.

Catching the knife by the blade results in misery and pain. Seizing it by the handle not only prevents a lot of anguish; it also prepares us for what comes next.

For some of us, what comes next is throwing the knife back. However, staying close to the heart of God reminds us that He has provided some marvelous resources to help us avoid getting "sliced" up by the adversities of life.

One of the best places to find those resources is God's Word. Take this one for example:

"I will take refuge in the shadow of your wings until the disaster has passed" (Psalm57:1b)

The Bible is to us what the star was to the wise men; but if we spend all our time in gazing upon it, observing its motions, and admiring its splendor, without being led to Christ by it, the use of it will be lost on us.

Thomas Adams

For whatever life holds for you and your family in the coming days, weave the unfailing fabric of God's Word through your heart and mind. It will hold strong, even if the rest of life unravels.

Gigi Graham Tchividjian

Your word, O Lord, is eternal;
it stands firm in the heavens.
Psalm 119:89

Diamonds on the Top

God's Word can be compared to a diamond field. Some of the gems are lying right on top of the ground. They are easy to spot and pick up. Others are to be found only after a lot of digging and searching out. We read in Psalm 119:162, "I rejoice in your promise like one who finds great spoil" (NIV).

God's Word can withstand the most careful scrutiny and examination. In fact, many of the wonders of Scriptures can be found only after careful scholarship. The very process of examination can open up new insights into His truth that we may have previously overlooked.

Never should it be used as a weapon to hurt or control others. Never should we search its sacred pages for support of a habit, attitude or lifestyle we've adopted, looking for an excuse to continue. The Bible says what it says.

William Gladstone called it an "impregnable rock." Roy Smith wrote, "More people are troubled by what is plain in Scripture than by what is obscure."

Obey what you do understand. Commit the rest of it to God. He can handle it.

There is no situation so chaotic
that God cannot from that situation,
create something that is surpassingly
good. He did it at the creation.
He did it at the cross.
He is doing it today.
Handley C. G. Moule

It is easy to sing when we can read the
notes by daylight; but he is the skillful
singer who can sing when there is not a
ray of light by which to read. . . .
Songs in the night come only from God;
they are not in the power of man.
Charles Haddon Spurgeon

The phrase "God is good" cannot be
reserved for those moments when life
turns out the way we had hoped.
Stacy and Paula Rinehart

*Sing and make music in your
heart to the Lord.*
Ephesians 5:19

Music from the Fire

Someone long ago wrote of sitting by a fire. The writer imagined the noises which came from the wood as it burned were imprisoned songs, finally brought to freedom by the flames.

The birds had sung while sitting on the branches of the tree. The wind had pushed its way through, making its own music. The rain had written a melody which sank deep into its roots. A child had played and sang in its shade. All these notes soaked into the wood, hidden away in the trunk.

They were hidden away until the flames set them free one evening chilly enough to warrant an open fire.

As the years pass, our spirits take in many different melodies of life. They may become trapped, hidden away by busyness, by apathy, by ignorance. The flames of adversity can serve as a wonderful tool in the Hands of God, releasing the music inside of us.

We don't have to just "pass through" life; we can gather songs along the way, storing them up for the day when we will need to hear them most.

In perplexities — when we cannot tell
what to do, when we cannot understand
what is going on around us — let us be
calmed and steadied and made patient
by the thought that what is hidden
from us is not hidden from Him.

Frances Ridley Havergal

Let us never forget that some of God's
greatest mercies are His refusals.
He says no in order that He may,
in some way we cannot imagine,
say yes. All His ways are merciful.
His meaning is always love.

Elisabeth Elliot

Whatever your circumstances may be,
rest assured that God does not
do things without a purpose.

Charles Stanley

Wait for the Lord, and He will deliver you.
Proverbs 20:22b

He Sometimes Says No

Have you ever had God say "no" to one of your most fervent prayers?

Ultimately, we must acknowledge that God has a purpose in allowing His children to suffer, even if we do not or cannot know what that purpose is. One unknown poet expressed it this way:

Humbly I asked of God to give me joy,
To crown my life with blossoms of delight:
I begged for happiness without alloy,
Discovering that my pathway should be bright.
Prayerfully I sought these blessings to attain
And now I thank Him that He gave me pain,
For with my pain and sorrow came to me
A dower of tenderness in act and thought,
And with the suffering came a sympathy
And insight that success had never brought.
Father, I had been foolish and unblest
If Thou hadst granted me my blind request.

Take a good look at those lines again. Then fall on your knees and thank God that sometimes He says, "No."

All of God's creatures are held
in the hands of His kindness.

Janet Weaver

God walks with us. He scoops us
up in His arms or simply sits with
us in silent strength until we cannot
avoid the awesome recognition that
yes, even now, He is here.

Gloria Gaither

Jesus is waiting for us in silence.
In that silence, He will listen to us,
there He will speak to our souls,
and there we will hear His voice.

Mother Teresa

*Call to me and I will answer you
and tell you great and unsearchable
things you do not know.*
Jeremiah 33:3

There is a God!

Brent D. Earles has written in *Psalms for Graduates:*

"The stars are God's fingerprints. The sun is a mere smidgen of his radiance. The moon is to remind us that he doesn't sleep at night. The vastness of space proclaims the infinity of his wisdom, while the sand pebble indicates his thoroughness with the puniest details. The lion hints at his fearlessness, the bear at his power, the hawk at his keen insight.

"And yet, those possess only a tidbit of God's omnipotence and omnipresence. Every tree points toward heaven; every bird has a song to sing; even every movement of wind goes in some direction. There is nothing chaotic about our beautiful designed world.

"All creation has a message to tell. It says, 'Listen, there is a God. There is a God!' "

No matter what happens or doesn't happen, remember that yes, there is a God.

And yes, He can definitely handle it.

Every day of our lives.

Now. Forever.

Quotations by Source

The words of the wise are like goads,
their collected sayings like firmly
embedded nails — given by one Shepherd.
Ecclesiastes 12:11

About the Author

Dr. S. M. Henriques, known to his friends as "Rocky," lives and writes in Jackson, Mississippi. He is a graduate of Mississippi College and New Orleans Baptist Theological Seminary, with 20 years' experience as a pastor.

Rocky is the author of *God Can Handle It . . . Marriage* and *God Can Handle It For Kids,* both published by Brighton Books. He is also publisher of *The Timothy Report,* an internet newsletter for pastors, church secretaries and Bible teachers.

Rocky and his wife Mary Ann are the parents of two children, Jennifer and Jonathan.

For information about *The Timothy Report,* address your e-mail to SwanLC@aol.com.

About Brighton Books

Brighton Books is a publisher of inspirational, Christian-based books. The company is located in Nashville, Tennessee. Brighton Books are distributed by Walnut Grove Press.

About the
"God Can Handle It" Series

This book is part of a series called *God Can Handle It*. Each book in this collection combines inspirational passages, meditations and relevant Scripture passages.

For more information about these or other titles from Brighton Books or Walnut Grove Press, please call 1-800-256-8584.